THE TIME-BLOCK PLANNER

SECOND EDITION

THE TIME-BLOCK PLANNER

SECOND EDITION

A Daily Method for Deep Work in a Distracted World

CAL NEWPORT

PORTFOLIO | PENGUIN

AUTHOR'S NOTE FOR THE SECOND EDITION

The Time-Block Planner was largely conceived and constructed during the fall of 2019 and early winter of 2020. At the time, I had no way of knowing that we were only a few short months away from a global pandemic that would radically destabilize our relationships with our jobs. The original intention of this tool was to help knowledge workers make progress on important objectives while simultaneously taming a deluge of incoming requests and tasks. It did, and still does, solve this problem well. The haphazard retreat to remote work induced by the pandemic, however, created a deeper issue. The boundaries between the professional and the personal dissolved, smearing together the frenetic demands of both into an unrelenting blend of anxious activity. It was in this mess that time blocking really shined. This method's insistence on creating your own trusted plan for your time, as opposed to simply reacting to whatever incoming demand happens to catch your attention, offered a sense of autonomy and calm within this otherwise destructive whirlwind. To be sure, *The Time-Block Planner* will help you get more done, but as many of its early users learned, it also provides you something equally powerful: control over the character and rhythm of your day. In early 2020 I'm not sure I fully grasped the importance of this latter goal. Today I absolutely do.

In the roughly three years that have passed since this planner was first released, I've received vast amounts of useful feedback generated from real-world field testing in many different professional contexts. This second edition of *The Time-Block Planner* integrates the best of this feedback. The most obvious change is the shift to spiral binding, which allows the planner to lay completely flat. This improves the experience of referencing your plan and processing notes. Another important change is the treatment of weekends and weekly planning. The first version of the planner provided two-page planning spreads for all seven days of the week, as well as two-page spreads for recording weekly plans. I realized, however, that I was increasingly advising people to *avoid* detailed schedules for weekend days, as it's beneficial to take regular breaks from the rigors of blocking. I also discovered that most people didn't need two full pages for weekly planning. Accordingly, in this new edition, I condensed both weekend and weekly planning into a single two-page spread. This freed up a significant number of pages, which I was able to then repurpose to include additional weeks in the planner, reducing the total number of planners needed to make it through a full year.

This may be a new edition of *The Time-Block Planner,* but it's unlikely to be the last. As I like to tell my readers and podcast listeners, when you buy this planner, you're not just buying a single notebook; you're buying into a planning *system.* As I continue to receive more feedback, I'll continue to tweak and improve the physical product. I'll also continue to offer updated advice for this method in both my email newsletter and podcast (see calnewport.com for more details). If you're new to time blocking, be prepared for your professional life to be transformed for the better. If you're already practiced at this skill, then I'm sure you'll enjoy these latest improvements. Either way, let's end things here with the valedictory phrase familiar to time blockers worldwide: "Shutdown complete."

Cal Newport
Takoma Park, MD
September 2022

INTRODUCTION

THE POWER OF TIME BLOCKING

The Time-Block Planner implements a personal productivity system that I've perfected over the past fifteen years. During this period, it helped me earn a PhD in computer science at MIT and then go on to achieve tenure as a professor at Georgetown University while simultaneously publishing seven books for general audiences, including multiple bestsellers. Most importantly—and one of the aspects that I believe sets my system apart from any other—I did all of this while rarely working past 5:30 p.m. I needed my evenings free to wrangle my three young kids. My productivity system made all this possible, and the planner you're currently holding will enable you to implement it in your own professional life.

As you'll learn in the detailed instructions that follow, the core of my system is a simple but powerful strategy called *time blocking.* Most people approach their workday by trying to cross things off a task list in the small slivers of time that remain between attending meetings and reacting to emails and instant messages. Time blocking, by contrast, requires you to figure out in advance how you want to spend every minute of your day. Instead of trying to generally "be productive," you partition your time into blocks and assign specific work to them. This critical shift from managing *tasks* to managing *time* can massively increase the amount of useful work you accomplish. It also provides an anxiety-reducing sense of control over your schedule.

I didn't invent time blocking. As soon as people began thinking seriously about personal productivity, they began preaching the benefits of this strategy. In his autobiography, Benjamin Franklin explains, "Every part of my business should have its allotted time." He then provides a sample time-block schedule that divides his waking hours into blocks, each dedicated to a different productive activity. In his 1967 classic, *The Effective Executive,* one of the first professional productivity books ever written, Peter Drucker echoes Franklin's commitment to managing time instead of tasks. "Effective executives, in my observation, do not start with their tasks," he writes. "They start with their time." A more recent article, appearing on a popular career website, reports that both Bill Gates and Elon Musk deploy variations of time blocking to help fuel their "freakish" levels of accomplishments.

This technique, in other words, is one that serious productivity aficionados have been deploying with great success for many years. This planner will help you follow their lead by providing you with the tools needed to design and execute your own effective time-block schedules. What you *won't* find in this planner is a substitute for your calendar. I assume you already manage your meetings and appointments elsewhere, such as the shared digital calendars that more and more organizations require their employees to use. Though you will copy events from your calendar into your daily time-block schedules, this planner is not their long-term home.

This planner also doesn't provide room for you to permanently store all of the various tasks and obligations for which you're currently responsible. The modern knowledge worker is burdened with many hundreds of these responsibilities at any given time; it's simply not practical to keep track of them in a paper notebook that's replaced multiple times a year. When using this planner, you will copy selected tasks from whatever system you use into your daily time-block schedules, but as with meetings and appointments, this will not be the primary place you store them.

The time-block planner instead focuses on a narrower objective: getting the most out of the time and attention you have available to allocate toward work each day. You already know what you need to do. This planner helps you do more of it, and do it more intentionally, than you ever thought possible. But enough with the preamble. Let's dive into the details of exactly how this planner works . . .

SHUTDOWN STATUS

METRIC TRACKING

COLLECTION

WEEK 1 DAY 1

Daily Metrics

shutdown complete ☐

TASKS:	IDEAS:

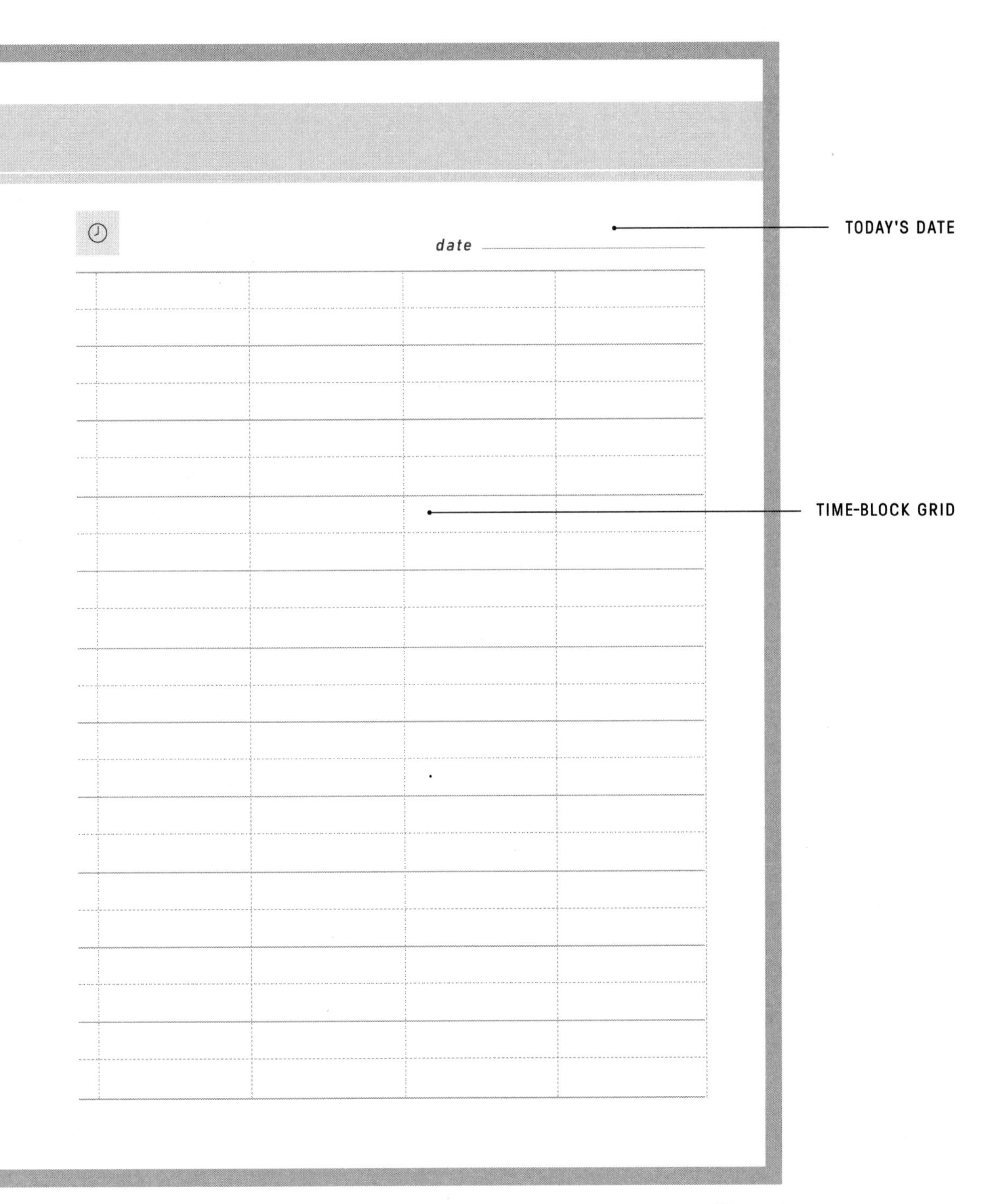

Figure 1

INSTRUCTIONS FOR USING THE TIME-BLOCK PLANNER

The time-block planner dedicates a two-page spread to each workday. I call these the *daily pages*. It also dedicates a two-page spread for each weekend that can be used to structure your Saturday and Sunday, and plan for the week ahead. I call these the *weekend pages*. We'll return to the weekend pages later in these instructions. For now, let's focus on the daily pages, as they're the key to this system's scheduling discipline.

As shown in figure 1, the daily pages contain several elements.

On the right-hand side is the time-block grid. This is where you'll maintain your time-block schedule for the given day. On the left-hand side is a pair of columns for collecting obligations or ideas that come up while you're in the middle of executing a time block. By writing these intrusions down in the moment to deal with later, you'll avoid the need to divert your attention. The left-hand side of the daily pages spread also includes a box dedicated to tracking metrics designed to measure behaviors that you identify as crucial to succeeding in your professional life. Inside this box is the "shutdown complete" checkbox that indicates that you've completed a shutdown ritual for the day. As you'll learn, this ritual has become a favorite of this system's devotees.

Let's walk through the use of these daily page elements one by one, starting with the most important, the time-block grid.

USING THE TIME-BLOCK GRID

At the beginning of each workday, flip to the next empty daily pages spread and record the date in the box at the top of the right-hand page. You're now ready to create a time-block schedule for the day. To do so, you'll use the time-block grid, also on the right-hand page. Each solid horizontal line represents one hour, and each dotted line represents a half hour.

9 finish report
10
(1)
11 research client x
12 lunch w. Sam
1
email
2
planning meeting
3
edit copy & shutdown
4

(1) Morning Tasks
- email triage
- submit form
- call Karen
- fill out doodle

Figure 2

Moving from the top to the bottom, label the solid lines on the left side of the page with the hours during which you plan to work during the day. For example, if you're working from 9:00 a.m. to 5:00 p.m., you'd label the first solid line 9:00, the second 10:00, and so on, down to 5:00.

You can now create a time-block schedule for these hours. When you build your first schedule for the day, use the first column of the grid. The other columns will be used later if you end up needing to fix your schedule as the day unfolds.

To build the schedule, partition your working hours into blocks of time and assign to each block the specific work you plan to accomplish during this time. You record this schedule on the time-block grid by actually drawing boxes around the time captured by each block and then labeling each with the work assigned to it. If you need more room for a block's description—for example, if you want to list out multiple tasks you plan to accomplish during a short block—put a number in the block, and then use that same number to label a list of the extra information in the upper right corner of the block grid, where it's unlikely to get in the way of future schedule fixes. To make these instructions concrete, see figure 2, which shows a sample time-block schedule.

When building your time-block schedule, you should first reference whatever calendar you use to make sure that you're adding time blocks for any meetings or appointments you already have scheduled. The real decision then becomes what to do with the free time that remains. To help make these choices, next consult whatever external system you use to track and organize all of the tasks, projects, long-term goals, or other obligations for which you're currently responsible. You want your schedule to help you make progress on the right activities.

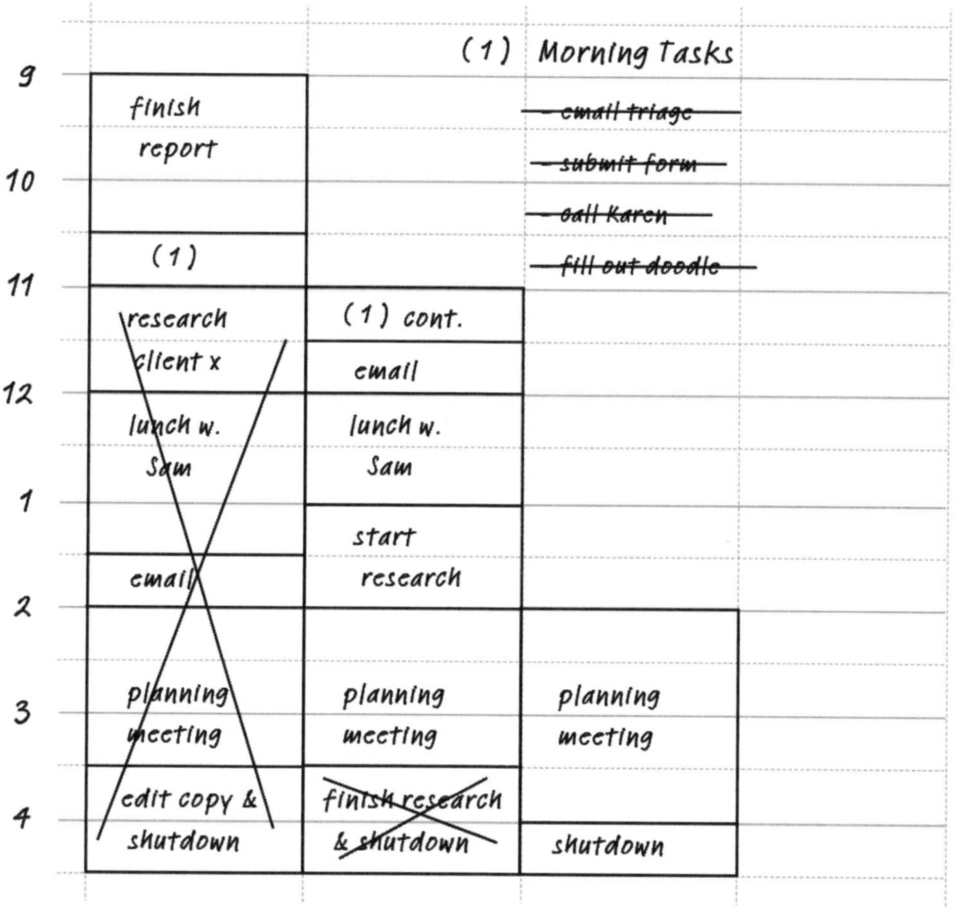

Figure 3

Finally, keep in mind factors such as time of day—perhaps earlier in the day is better for hard thinking and later in the day is better for small tasks—and how you're feeling.

If you're exhausted, you might want a schedule designed to help you catch up on administrative obligations, whereas if you're feeling energized, you might want to put aside large blocks of uninterrupted time for intense projects.

As your day unfolds, you should use your time-block schedule to determine what work you should be doing at any given moment. It's important that you don't let your attention wander. Focus exclusively on the work scheduled for the current block until the block is completed. If you need breaks, schedule them.

It's unavoidable, of course, that you'll occasionally deviate from your current schedule. For example, maybe a given task took longer than expected, or your boss asked you to stop everything to tackle a new urgent assignment. In these cases, you don't abandon your time-block schedule, you instead *fix* it whenever you next get the chance. To make this fix, first cross out the time blocks that remain in your current schedule. Then, in the next column to the right of your current schedule, create a new schedule for these remaining hours and turn your attention to executing this new plan. If this revised schedule breaks at some point, then repeat the same fixing process: cross out the blocks that remain and schedule new blocks for this time in the next column to the right. And so on. Figure 3 shows an example of this schedule-fixing process in action.

Notice that it's possible to instead craft your block schedule using pencil and then fix it by erasing and redrawing the blocks in the same column. I generally avoid this method for two reasons: the erasing and redrawing can get messy, and I like to have a record of the changes I made, as these can later help me identify recurring scheduling mistakes.

ADVANCED TIME-BLOCKING TIPS

Tip #1: Embrace schedule fixes.

The goal of time blocking is not to stick to your original schedule no matter what. It's instead to try to always have an intentional plan for what to do with your time. If circumstances upend your schedule, this isn't a failure, it's an expected part of applying this strategy. When you next get a chance, simply fix the schedule for the time that remains in the day so that you remain intentional about where you direct your focus.

Tip #2: At first, schedule more time than you think you need.

Novice time blockers chronically underestimate how long common work activities actually take. If you're new to time blocking, you can save yourself unnecessary schedule fixes by inflating the time-block sizes you think are reasonable by 20 to 30 percent. After you've been time blocking for several months, you'll begin to develop a more realistic understanding of these durations and can begin building more-accurate blocks without needing this extra padding.

Tip #3: Capture email and instant messenger communication in their own blocks.

Many knowledge workers don't consider checking email or instant messenger channels a standalone activity. They instead think of it as something that's always done in parallel with primary work. I *highly* discourage this mindset: all of these quick checks of communication channels significantly reduce your cognitive capacity due to neural network switching costs. Batch your email or instant messenger time into their own blocks. When you get to one of these communication blocks, do nothing but communicate, and when you're not in one of these blocks, don't communicate at all. If your work requires you to check these tools often, then schedule lots of blocks to do so, but refuse to let this behavior be something that occurs informally in the background.

Tip #4: Use "conditional blocks" to add flexibility to your schedule.

If you're unsure how long a given activity might take, break it into two blocks. The first block is dedicated to working on the activity. The activity for the second block is conditioned on what happens during the first block: If you need more time for the original activity, then the second block is used to finish it. On the other hand, if you've finished the original activity, the second block can be used to tackle a backup task. In this way, you can avoid unnecessary schedule fixes when confronting work of ambiguous duration.

USING THE COLLECTION COLUMNS

On the left-hand side of the daily pages are two lined columns labeled "tasks" and "ideas." Their purpose is simple: if while you're executing your time-block schedule you come across a new task or relevant idea, you can jot it down in these collection columns to deal with later, and then return immediately to executing the current block.

For example, perhaps someone sticks their head into your office to ask you to do something for them, or while walking back from a meeting, you have a sudden brainstorm about how to tackle a pressing problem. By writing down these cognitive intrusions in a designated area in this planner, you avoid the need to divert your attention from the current time block to handle them in the moment. You can be confident that they won't be forgotten, as they're written right there in black and white on your daily pages. If you're without such a collection space, the fear of forgetting would likely drive you to drop everything to handle the new obligation right away, a reaction that cedes control of your schedule from your intentions to the whims of other people.

If you need to take action on this new information later the same day, then the collection columns will hold it for you until you arrive at a good time to fix your time-block schedule to include this work. If the information is less urgent, then it will remain safely recorded in the collection columns until you complete your shutdown ritual at the end of the day (we'll get to this soon), during which you'll transfer it to whatever permanent system you use to track your obligations. If a new idea or task arrives *after* you have completed your shutdown ritual for the current day, you jot it down in the collection columns for the next day, where you are sure to see it when you create that day's plan.

METRIC TRACKING

Part of the art of time blocking is figuring out what work to schedule. Some of these choices are obvious, like allocating blocks for preexisting appointments or projects with impending deadlines. But you'll still often find yourself needing to schedule more discretionary, non-urgent endeavors. It's here that personal metrics can help nudge you toward the long-term results that matter most to you.

A personal metric describes a behavior that you think is important with a quantifiable value. Many readers of my book *Deep Work*, for example, track how many hours they spent working without distractions on cognitively demanding tasks each day. They accept my argument that this "deep work" should be prioritized in an increasingly competitive knowledge economy. Their daily deep work hour count is a personal metric that captures how well they're living up to this commitment.

Some jobs might yield metrics that capture behaviors specific to the particular type of work. If you're in sales, for example, the number of sales calls you make each day might be important, while if you're in a leadership position, you might instead want to track how many different team members you checked in on during the day. Some metrics are quantified as numbers, while others are binary: you either did them or you didn't. Perhaps, for example, you maintain a simple checkbox to indicate whether you ended the day with an empty inbox or filled out your online time sheet.

You can also track personal metrics that are only loosely relevant to your work. In my own case, for example, I'm a strong believer that a healthy body supports a healthy mind. Accordingly, each day I track the following information: how many steps I take, whether or not I exercised, and whether or not I ate healthily. These personal metrics aren't, strictly speaking, describing work activities, but I track them alongside more work-specific values, as they ultimately do affect how much useful thinking I'm able to extract from my brain.

The open box above the collection columns is the space for recording these types of metrics each day. You simply jot down the name of each metric followed by the relevant value—be it a number, a tally of hash marks, or a simple check. Tracking personal metrics serves a couple of purposes. The first is psychological. The knowledge that you'll be recording information about a key behavior at the end of the day can motivate you to dedicate time to that behavior when building your time-block schedule, as you don't want to have to record a disappointing metric value.

The second purpose is informational. The metric tracking boxes will contain a record of how well you did, day after day, in executing key behaviors. This record can reveal useful trends. For example, if you're tracking deep work hours, you might notice that these values dip precipitously on Tuesdays and Thursdays. Further investigation might reveal this is because you have a series of regular meetings on those days that are spread out enough throughout the day to break up any long, uninterrupted stretches of time. Once the problem is identified, simple fixes might be possible. In this case, perhaps you reschedule one of the meetings to free up a morning block for deep work on these days.

To summarize, if something's important to you, track it in the metric-tracking box. This simple habit can inject much more intentional behavior into your daily schedule.

THE SHUTDOWN RITUAL

One of the most important pieces of my system's daily scheduling discipline is executing a shutdown ritual that helps your mind shift more completely from work mode to non-work mode. The details of this ritual are straightforward. At the end of each day's time-block schedule, your final step, if at all possible, is to shut down work. To do so, first make sure your personal metrics have been recorded. Next, go through the tasks and ideas in your collection columns, deciding for each what you want to do with it. In some cases, you may need to add new tasks into your task system, while in others, you may need to update your calendar or even shoot off a quick message.

Once you've finished going through your collection columns, you should then briefly review any other potential sources of unresolved work obligations. For most people, this means taking one last look at your email inbox, to ensure you didn't miss something urgent, as well as reviewing your calendar and obligation-tracking system. When done with these checks, look over your weekly plan (which we'll discuss in more detail next), updating it as needed. The goal here is to convince yourself that there's nothing being forgotten or missed or being kept track of only in your brain, and that you have a reasonable plan for the days ahead. All of these reassurances are the precondition for enabling your brain to fully shift its attention from work to life outside work.

To make this transition, complete the shutdown ritual by marking the "shutdown complete" checkbox that's preprinted in the metric-tracking space. (I put this checkbox in the metric area because recording whether or not you've completed this ritual is itself a personal metric.) Later in the evening, if you feel a generalized background hum of work anxiety and your mind begins to fret and wants you to think about that email you have to write, or to endlessly review your plan for an upcoming project, you can arrest this rumination with a simple reminder: "I wouldn't have checked the shutdown complete box if I hadn't completed the shutdown ritual that convinced me I'm fine to avoid work until tomorrow." In this way, you address the anxiety without engaging with the specific topics fueling the anxiety.

THE WEEKEND PAGES

So far in these instructions, we've been discussing the various elements of the daily planning pages, which are meant to help you control your time Monday through Friday. Every week's worth of daily pages is also accompanied by a two-page weekend spread. As shown in figure 4, the page on the left is dedicated to organizing Saturday and Sunday, while the page on the right is for capturing your weekly plan, a high-level road map for the week ahead. We will discuss both in more detail.

Time blocking is effective but it can also be exhausting, which is why I typically advise people not to time block their weekends: these two days should provide some respite from the rigors of allocating work to every minute of your day. This is why the planner provides only a single page for organizing your entire weekend. The page is divided into two columns, one for Saturday and one for Sunday. The empty boxes included for each day can be used for jotting down a loose schedule, including reminders of any important appointments ("Dinner with the Smiths at 7:00") or major things you hope to get done ("Mow the lawn"). These boxes can also be used to collect daily metrics, assuming your metric tracking habit extends to the weekend. The lined space below these boxes that's labeled "Weekend Capture" should be used for capturing ideas or tasks that come up on Saturday or Sunday. I suggest you always process these notes when you create your time-block plan on Monday morning. This will ensure that they're never forgotten.

The right-hand side of the weekend pages includes space for you to plan the upcoming week. This area is purposefully left simple. When it comes to weekly planning, I've found it's crucial to embrace flexibility. The style or format of your plan should match the challenges of the specific week ahead.

Regardless of the format you use, you should work out your weekly plan either first thing Monday morning or over the weekend before the week begins. When crafting the plan, look over your calendar and whatever system you use to track your obligations, projects, and goals. Some people like to empty their email inbox as part of this planning process so that they feel as though they're

SATURDAY

SUNDAY

WEEKEND CAPTURE

WEEKLY PLAN

We spend much of our day on autopilot—not giving much thought to what we're doing with our time. This is a problem. It's difficult to prevent the trivial from creeping into every corner of your schedule if you don't face, without flinching, your current balance between deep and shallow work, and then adopt the habit of pausing before taking action and asking, "What makes the most sense right now?"

Figure 4

starting the week fresh. For other people, this might be infeasible. Regardless, creating these plans takes time. For example, I usually spend between thirty and sixty minutes to get up to speed on what's happening in the upcoming week and decide how to tackle it.

You might feel at first that this time is wasted—like you're throwing away an hour you could dedicate to actually completing concrete tasks. I urge you to resist this reaction. The planning may take time up front, but it will return much greater productivity for the entire week that follows. Among other benefits, it will allow you to identify important patterns that can help you get much more accomplished. If you see, for example, that Wednesday through Friday are very busy due to a visiting client, then you can compensate by squeezing in more uninterrupted deep work on Monday or Tuesday. Or if you know you'll be off-site all day Friday, then you can adjust your Thursday schedule to make sure loose ends are tied up before the trip.

Sometimes your weekly planning habit can motivate you to change appointments already on your calendar. After trying and failing to fit in enough hours to finish an important project, for example, you might realize that you need to cancel or reschedule a few non-urgent appointments—perhaps coffee with a colleague or a brainstorming meeting for a speculative project—to make room for the more urgent work.

Weekly plans are also important because they allow you to tackle objectives that require more than a day to complete. If you decide at the beginning of the week, for example, to write an article that'll require around ten to fifteen hours of research and writing, your weekly plan can help you figure out how to spread this work out across the upcoming days. It's much less likely you'd end up getting all of this required work done if you instead just planned each day as it arrived.

It's this combination of high-level weekly plans with detailed daily time-block schedules that unlocks the full potential of this productivity system. The weekly/daily approach is what allows you to begin moving obligations around like pieces on a chessboard, and to construct configurations of your schedule that enable you to accomplish head-turning amounts of work, all while staying on top of the various small requests and tasks pulling at your time and attention. While your peers react frantically to inputs and deadlines as they arise, often putting in late nights to try to compensate for their haphazard schedules, you'll approach each day with a justified confidence.

Build smart weekly plans. Use this plan to develop effective daily time-block schedules. Execute those daily schedules with intensity. When you're done for the day, shut down completely. When you get to the weekend, take a break from rigorous scheduling. Then start the cycle all over again. This is the rhythm of a professional life that's both extremely productive and sustainable. And it's exactly what this planner is designed to help you achieve.

WEEK 1 **DAY 1**

Daily Metrics

shutdown complete ☐

TASKS:	IDEAS:

date

WEEK 1 DAY 2

Daily Metrics

shutdown complete ☐

TASKS:	IDEAS:

date ______________________

WEEK 1 **DAY 3**

Daily Metrics

shutdown complete ☐

TASKS:	IDEAS:

date

WEEK 1 **DAY 4**

Daily Metrics

shutdown complete ☐

TASKS:	**IDEAS:**

date

WEEK 1 **DAY 5**

Daily Metrics

shutdown complete ☐

TASKS:	IDEAS:

date ______________________________

SATURDAY

SUNDAY

WEEKEND CAPTURE

WEEKLY PLAN

We spend much of our day on autopilot—not giving much thought to what we're doing with our time. This is a problem. It's difficult to prevent the trivial from creeping into every corner of your schedule if you don't face, without flinching, your current balance between deep and shallow work, and then adopt the habit of pausing before taking action and asking, "What makes the most sense right now?"

WEEK 2 DAY 1

Daily Metrics

shutdown complete ☐

TASKS:	IDEAS:

date ______

WEEK 2 DAY 2

Daily Metrics

shutdown complete ☐

TASKS:	IDEAS:

date ______

WEEK 2 DAY 3

Daily Metrics

shutdown complete ☐

TASKS:	IDEAS:

date

WEEK 2 **DAY 4**

Daily Metrics

shutdown complete ☐

TASKS:	IDEAS:

date ______________________

WEEK 2 DAY 5

Daily Metrics

shutdown complete ☐

TASKS:	IDEAS:

date

SATURDAY

SUNDAY

WEEKEND CAPTURE

WEEKLY PLAN

Few people want to spend so much time online, but social media apps and websites have a way of cultivating behavioral addictions. The urge to check Twitter or refresh Reddit becomes a nervous twitch that shatters uninterrupted time into shards too small to support the presence necessary for an intentional life. This reality must be resisted.

WEEK 3 **DAY 1**

Daily Metrics

shutdown complete ☐

TASKS:	IDEAS:

date ______________________

WEEK 3 **DAY 2**

Daily Metrics

shutdown complete ☐

TASKS:	IDEAS:

date ______________________

WEEK 3 DAY 3

Daily Metrics

shutdown complete ☐

TASKS:	IDEAS:

date ______________________

WEEK 3 DAY 4

Daily Metrics

shutdown complete ☐

TASKS:	IDEAS:

date ______________________

WEEK 3 DAY 5

Daily Metrics

shutdown complete ☐

TASKS:	IDEAS:

date ______

SATURDAY

SUNDAY

WEEKEND CAPTURE

WEEKLY PLAN

Shallow work is inevitable, but you must keep it confined to a point where it doesn't impede your ability to take full advantage of the deeper efforts that ultimately determine your impact.

WEEK 4 DAY 1

Daily Metrics

shutdown complete ☐

TASKS:	IDEAS:

date

WEEK 4 DAY 2

Daily Metrics

shutdown complete ☐

TASKS:	IDEAS:

date ____________________

WEEK 4 DAY 3

Daily Metrics

shutdown complete ☐

TASKS:	IDEAS:

date ____________________

WEEK 4 DAY 4

Daily Metrics

shutdown complete ☐

TASKS:	IDEAS:

date ______________________

WEEK 4 DAY 5

Daily Metrics

shutdown complete ☐

TASKS:	IDEAS:

date

SATURDAY

SUNDAY

WEEKEND CAPTURE

WEEKLY PLAN

When you attempt to maintain multiple ongoing electronic conversations while also working on a primary task like writing a report or coding a computer program, your prefrontal cortex must continually jump back and forth between different goals. This *network switching* is not an instantaneous process; it requires both time and cognitive resources. When you try to do it rapidly, things get messy.

WEEK 5 DAY 1

Daily Metrics

shutdown complete ☐

TASKS:	IDEAS:

date

WEEK 5 DAY 2

Daily Metrics

shutdown complete ☐

TASKS:	IDEAS:

date ____________________

WEEK 5 **DAY 3**

Daily Metrics

shutdown complete ☐

TASKS:	IDEAS:

date

WEEK 5 **DAY 4**

Daily Metrics

shutdown complete ☐

TASKS:	IDEAS:

date ______

WEEK 5 DAY 5

Daily Metrics

shutdown complete ☐

TASKS:	IDEAS:

date ______________________

SATURDAY

SUNDAY

WEEKEND CAPTURE

WEEKLY PLAN

Having deadlines and obligations floating around in your mind is exhausting—it makes it impossible to completely relax and, over time, can lead you down the path toward a breakdown. However, once you figure out what work needs to be done and when, it's like a weight being lifted from your shoulders. The uncertainty vanishes: when you work, you can fully concentrate on the assignment in front of you, and when you relax, you can do so without any anxiety.

WEEK 6 DAY 1

Daily Metrics

shutdown complete ☐

TASKS:	IDEAS:

date ____________________

WEEK 6 **DAY 2**

Daily Metrics

shutdown complete ☐

TASKS:	IDEAS:

date ______________

WEEK 6 **DAY 3**

Daily Metrics

shutdown complete ☐

TASKS:	IDEAS:

date ______________________

WEEK 6 DAY 4

Daily Metrics

shutdown complete ☐

TASKS:	IDEAS:

date

WEEK 6 DAY 5

Daily Metrics

shutdown complete ☐

TASKS:	IDEAS:

date

SATURDAY

SUNDAY

WEEKEND CAPTURE

WEEKLY PLAN

Your goal is not to stick to a given schedule at all costs; it's instead to maintain, at all times, a thoughtful say in what you're doing with your time going forward—even if these decisions are reworked again and again as the day unfolds.

WEEK 7 DAY 1

Daily Metrics

shutdown complete ☐

TASKS:	IDEAS:

date ______________________

WEEK 7 DAY 2

Daily Metrics

shutdown complete ☐

TASKS:	IDEAS:

date

WEEK 7 DAY 3

Daily Metrics

shutdown complete ☐

TASKS:	IDEAS:

date

WEEK 7 DAY 4

Daily Metrics

shutdown complete ☐

TASKS:	IDEAS:

date

WEEK 7 **DAY 5**

Daily Metrics

shutdown complete ☐

TASKS:	IDEAS:

date ______

SATURDAY

SUNDAY

WEEKEND CAPTURE

WEEKLY PLAN

Thoreau once wrote, "I think that I cannot preserve my health and spirits, unless I spend four hours a day at least—and it is commonly more than that—sauntering through the woods and over the hills and fields, absolutely free from all worldly engagements." Most of us will never meet Thoreau's ambitious commitment to ambulation. But if we remain inspired by his vision, and try to spend as much time as is reasonable on foot and engaging in the "noble art" of walking, we, too, will experience success in preserving our health and spirits.

WEEK 8 DAY 1

Daily Metrics

shutdown complete ☐

TASKS:	IDEAS:

date

WEEK 8 DAY 2

Daily Metrics

shutdown complete ☐

TASKS:	IDEAS:

date ______________________

WEEK 8 DAY 3

Daily Metrics

shutdown complete ☐

TASKS:	IDEAS:

date ______________________

WEEK 8 DAY 4

Daily Metrics

shutdown complete ☐

TASKS:	IDEAS:

date ____________________

WEEK 8 DAY 5

Daily Metrics

shutdown complete ☐

TASKS:	IDEAS:

date

SATURDAY

SUNDAY

WEEKEND CAPTURE

WEEKLY PLAN

When you reduce work to a state of nature by allowing processes to unfold informally, the resulting behavior is anything but utopian.

WEEK 9 DAY 1

Daily Metrics

shutdown complete ☐

TASKS:	IDEAS:

date ______________________

WEEK 9 DAY 2

Daily Metrics

shutdown complete ☐

TASKS:	IDEAS:

date ______________________

WEEK 9 DAY 3

Daily Metrics

shutdown complete ☐

TASKS:	IDEAS:

date

WEEK 9 **DAY 4**

Daily Metrics

shutdown complete ☐

TASKS:	IDEAS:

date ________________

WEEK 9 DAY 5

Daily Metrics

shutdown complete ☐

TASKS:	IDEAS:

date __________

SATURDAY

SUNDAY

WEEKEND CAPTURE

WEEKLY PLAN

If you overestimate your free time, then you are likely to put off work until it's too late. And this leads to all-nighters, panic attacks, and shoddy performance. A realistic sense of time is arguably one of the most important factors in succeeding.

WEEK 10 DAY 1

Daily Metrics

shutdown complete ☐

TASKS:	IDEAS:

date

WEEK 10 **DAY 2**

Daily Metrics

shutdown complete ☐

TASKS:	IDEAS:

date ______________________

WEEK 10 DAY 3

Daily Metrics

shutdown complete ☐

TASKS:	IDEAS:

date ______

WEEK 10 **DAY 4**

Daily Metrics

shutdown complete ☐

TASKS:	IDEAS:

date

WEEK 10 DAY 5

Daily Metrics

shutdown complete ☐

TASKS:	IDEAS:

date ______________________

SATURDAY

SUNDAY

WEEKEND CAPTURE

WEEKLY PLAN

Sometimes people ask if the structured nature of time blocking will stifle creativity. I understand this concern, but it's fundamentally misguided. If you control your schedule: (1) you can ensure that you consistently dedicate time to the deep efforts that matter for creative pursuits; and (2) the stress relief that comes from this sense of organization allows you to go deeper into your creative blocks and produce more value.

WEEK 11 DAY 1

Daily Metrics

shutdown complete ☐

TASKS:	IDEAS:

date ____________________

WEEK 11 DAY 2

Daily Metrics

shutdown complete ☐

TASKS:	IDEAS:

date

WEEK 11 **DAY 3**

Daily Metrics

shutdown complete ☐

TASKS:	IDEAS:

date ______

WEEK 11 DAY 4

Daily Metrics

shutdown complete ☐

TASKS:	IDEAS:

date ______________________

WEEK 11 DAY 5

Daily Metrics

shutdown complete ☐

TASKS:	IDEAS:

date

SATURDAY

SUNDAY

WEEKEND CAPTURE

WEEKLY PLAN

The key to developing a deep work habit is to move beyond good intentions and add routines and rituals to your working life designed to minimize the amount of your limited willpower that is necessary to transition into and maintain a state of unbroken concentration.

WEEK 12 DAY 1

Daily Metrics

shutdown complete ☐

TASKS:	IDEAS:

date ______________________

WEEK 12 DAY 2

Daily Metrics

shutdown complete ☐

TASKS:	IDEAS:

date ______________________

WEEK 12 DAY 3

Daily Metrics

shutdown complete ☐

TASKS:	IDEAS:

date ______________________

WEEK 12 DAY 4

Daily Metrics

shutdown complete ☐

TASKS:	IDEAS:

date ________________

WEEK 12 DAY 5

Daily Metrics

shutdown complete ☐

TASKS:	IDEAS:

date ____________________

SATURDAY SUNDAY

WEEKEND CAPTURE

WEEKLY PLAN

When we made communication easier with tools like email, we accidently triggered a massive increase in our relative workloads. There's nothing fundamental about these newly increased workloads; they're instead an unintended side effect—a source of stress and anxiety that we can diminish if we're willing to step away from the frenetic back-and-forth that defines the modern workplace.

WEEK 13 DAY 1

Daily Metrics

shutdown complete ☐

TASKS:	IDEAS:

date

WEEK 13 **DAY 2**

Daily Metrics

shutdown complete ☐

TASKS:	IDEAS:

date ______________________________

WEEK 13 DAY 3

Daily Metrics

shutdown complete ☐

TASKS:	IDEAS:

date

WEEK 13 **DAY 4**

Daily Metrics

shutdown complete ☐

TASKS:	IDEAS:

date

WEEK 13 DAY 5

Daily Metrics

shutdown complete ☐

TASKS:	IDEAS:

date ____________________

SATURDAY

SUNDAY

WEEKEND CAPTURE

WEEKLY PLAN

In an age of network tools, knowledge workers increasingly replace deep work with the shallow alternative—constantly sending and receiving email messages like human network routers, with frequent breaks for quick hits of distraction. Larger efforts that would be well served by deep thinking, such as forming a new business strategy or writing an important grant application, get fragmented into distracted dashes that produce muted quality.

WEEK 14 DAY 1

Daily Metrics

shutdown complete ☐

TASKS:	IDEAS:

date ______________________

WEEK 14 DAY 2

Daily Metrics

shutdown complete ☐

TASKS:	IDEAS:

date

WEEK 14 **DAY 3**

Daily Metrics

shutdown complete ☐

TASKS:	IDEAS:

date ____________________

WEEK 14 **DAY 4**

Daily Metrics

shutdown complete ☐

TASKS:	IDEAS:

date ______________________

WEEK 14 DAY 5

Daily Metrics

shutdown complete ☐

TASKS:	IDEAS:

date ______________________

SATURDAY SUNDAY

WEEKEND CAPTURE

WEEKLY PLAN

I take time blocking seriously. My goal is to make sure progress is being made on the right things at the right pace for the relevant deadlines. This type of planning, to me, is like a chess game, with blocks of work getting strategically moved around in such a way that projects big and small all seem to fall into place with (just enough) time to spare.

WEEK 15 DAY 1

Daily Metrics

shutdown complete ☐

TASKS:	IDEAS:

date

WEEK 15 DAY 2

Daily Metrics

shutdown complete ☐

TASKS:	IDEAS:

date

WEEK 15 DAY 3

Daily Metrics

shutdown complete ☐

TASKS:	IDEAS:

date ______________________

WEEK 15 DAY 4

Daily Metrics

shutdown complete ☐

TASKS:	IDEAS:

date ______________________

WEEK 15 **DAY 5**

Daily Metrics

shutdown complete ☐

TASKS:	IDEAS:

date

SATURDAY

SUNDAY

WEEKEND CAPTURE

WEEKLY PLAN

Inspired, I turned my attention to a habit that continues to this day: I track the hours spent each month working deeply on hard problems. This hour-tracking strategy helped turn my attention back above all else to the quality of what I produce.

WEEK 16 DAY 1

Daily Metrics

shutdown complete ☐

TASKS:	IDEAS:

date

WEEK 16 **DAY 2**

Daily Metrics

shutdown complete ☐

TASKS:	IDEAS:

date ______________________

WEEK 16 DAY 3

Daily Metrics

shutdown complete ☐

TASKS:	IDEAS:

date

WEEK 16 DAY 4

Daily Metrics

shutdown complete ☐

TASKS:	IDEAS:

date

WEEK 16 **DAY 5**

Daily Metrics

shutdown complete ☐

TASKS:	IDEAS:

date ______________________________

SATURDAY

SUNDAY

WEEKEND CAPTURE

WEEKLY PLAN

When asked what one skill was most important to earn straight As, without becoming a grind, the students I interviewed cited the ability to get work done quickly and with a minimum of wasted effort. So how do they achieve this goal? A big part of the solution is timing—they gain efficiency by compressing work into focused bursts. To understand the power of this approach, consider the following simple formula: work accomplished = time spent × intensity of focus.

PROCESS AND PROCEED

You've made it through sixteen weeks of time blocking. Hopefully, you felt more productive and more in control of your work during this period. Before moving on to a fresh planner for the next sixteen weeks, however, it's important to take some time to process what you've learned. I suggest browsing through the pages of your planner to review the following information:

- **Metric Completion.** Survey your metrics to develop a better picture of your activity during these weeks. If you track deep work hours, for example, this is a good time to confront how many such hours you completed on average. If you're not happy with this number, perhaps it's time to consider more serious changes to your work setup. Similarly, if you find that you're struggling to complete a given metric, you might tweak the behavior you're tracking to something more tractable.

- **Schedule Repairs.** Review the days where your time-block schedule required multiple repairs. Study the source of these disruptions. It might turn out, for example, that you chronically underestimate the time required for a certain work activity. This is useful to know! If the disruption is external—say, your boss has the habit of stopping by your office to ask you to "quickly look into" their latest big idea—it might make sense to put a process in place that allows you to handle these requests without blowing up your schedule.

- **Time Allocation.** More generally, as you look over your recent time-block schedules, improve your understanding of how you actually spend your time. Are your days almost universally fractured with meetings? What's your ratio of email to non-email efforts? Most knowledge workers never directly confront the reality of their professional efforts, but such confrontation is crucial, even if it can sometimes be uncomfortable. To move from busy to effective, you must understand exactly how you're *actually* spending your time, identify what you don't like about these allocations, and then take hard steps to fix them.

Once you've reviewed and processed this information, you're prepared to start fresh with a new planner, armed with knowledge that will make you an even more effective time blocker than before. When it comes to your work life, if you don't control your time, others will do it for you. I hope your experience with time blocking so far has helped you appreciate the superiority of the first option.

Portfolio / Penguin
An imprint of Penguin Random House LLC
penguinrandomhouse.com

This edition with an updated introduction and interior published in 2023

Quotations that appear in this work originally appeared, some in different form, in *Digital Minimalism, Deep Work, So Good They Can't Ignore You, How to Become a Straight-A Student, A World Without Email* and on the author's blog, *Study Hacks*.

Library of Congress Cataloging-in-Publication Data

ISBN 9780593545393 (trade)

Printed in India
1 3 5 7 9 10 8 6 4 2

Book design by Lucia Bernard and Meighan Cavanaugh